IN THIS SERIES

THE COMPOSITE GUIDE

to LACROSSE

LOIS NICHOLSON

CHELSEA HOUSE PUBLISHERS
Philadelphia

Produced by Choptank Syndicate, Inc.

Editor and Picture Researcher: Norman L. Macht
Production Coordinator and Editorial Assistant: Mary E. Hull
Design and Production: Lisa Hochstein
Cover Illustrator: Cliff Spohn
Cover Design: Keith Trego
Art Direction: Sara Davis

The author is grateful to Julia Mignatti, Director
of Programs and Services of The Lacrosse Foundation
of Baltimore for her invaluable assistance.

The Chelsea House World Wide Web address is
http://www.chelseahouse.com

3 5 7 9 8 6 4

Library of Congress Cataloging-in-Publication Data

Nicholson, Lois, 1949-
      The composite guide to lacrosse / Lois Nicholson.
          p.   cm.— (The composite guide)
      Includes bibliographical references (p.) and index.
      Summary: Traces the history of this game from the time it was played
by North American Indians to its current popularity from elementary
schools to professional and international levels.
      ISBN 0-7910-4719-9 (hardcover)
      1. Lacrosse—Juvenile literature. 2. Lacrosse—History—Juvenile literature.
3. Indians of North America—Games—Juvenile Literature.
[1. Lacrosse. 2. Indians of North America—Games.] I. Title. II. Series.
GV989.N53 1998
796.34'7—dc21   98-13891
                                                                          CIP
                                                                          AC

CONTENTS

1

"WE COULDN'T STOP THEM"

The Princeton Tigers were hungry. It had been 49 years since they had tasted a national collegiate lacrosse championship. After winning a second title in three years back in 1953, the one-time kings of the turf had fallen on lean times.

Their record of 2–13 in 1988 was typical of the sorry state that Princeton lacrosse had fallen into, while Syracuse, North Carolina, and Johns Hopkins were winning every championship since 1977.

But coach Bill Tierney, a former Hopkins assistant, had built a contender around midfielders Andy Moe and Greg Waller, defender Mike Mariano, and attackman Justin Tortolani. In 1991 he added Scott Bacigalupo, the best high school goalie in the state of Maryland. That year they made the NCAA playoffs, pushing Towson State to triple overtime before losing 14–13 in the quarterfinals.

In 1992 they made it to the finals, but standing in the way of their long journey back to the top was perennial powerhouse Syracuse. The Orangemen, coached by Roy Simmons Jr., were used to winning, having captured three straight titles 1988–1990. But they had failed to reach the finals the past two years. Always hungry for victory, they roared into the 1992 tournament and devoured Yale, 17–8, defending champion North Carolina, 16–14, and Hopkins, 21–16, on a 7-point roll in the last six minutes. The 37-point

Princeton defenseman Dave Morrow (17) and goalie Scott Bacigalupo combine to stop Syracuse attackman Matt Riter in a 1993 NCAA semifinal. Princeton won four championships between 1992 and 1997.

one-game total score set an NCAA tournament record, topping Syracuse's 28–7 romp over the University of Massachusetts a year earlier.

After the semifinal, a stunned Hopkins coach Tony Seaman said, "We missed a give and go and they went down to the other end and scored. They had a run. We knew they were going to make it. The whole world knew they were going to make it. They made it and we couldn't stop them."

"We're an explosive team," said Syracuse coach Simmons, "and if we play our game, we're tough to beat."

So the powerful Orangeman faced off against the starving Tigers at Franklin Field in Philadelphia on Memorial Day weekend. Princeton's strategy relied on fresh legs (in a semifinal against North Carolina they had used 26 players in the first quarter) and a methodical offense designed to control the ball and eat up the clock. But when they had to, they could turn up the tempo.

Despite losing six of 10 face-offs, Princeton outplayed Syracuse in the first half. Led by Andy Moe's three goals, they ran up a 7–2 lead while limiting Syracuse to just 14 shots. A tight defense led by David Morrow and goalie Scott Bacigalupo shut them down. Pressing to overcome Princeton's slow pace and ball control, the frustrated Syracuse players missed catches and threw wildly.

As the second half began, the crowd confidently anticipated the usual Syracuse explosion. It would just be a matter of time, they knew. But Princeton scored first, at 5:13 of the third quarter, to make it 8–2.

Then the lightning struck. Syracuse ran off 6 points in 10 minutes to tie the game. To

Tigers goalie Scott Bacigalupo, it seemed as if a hail storm had hit him. "I kept telling myself to hang in there, to keep making saves," he said later. "I had told people that, if we could keep them to nine goals, we could win."

Princeton stopped the blitz long enough to regain the lead, 9–8, when Greg Waller scored an unassisted goal with 2:37 left on the clock. They kept the pressure on Syracuse goalie Chris Surran. With less than a minute to play, Surran picked up the ball and hurled it down-field. Bacigalupo came out from the goal and picked it up, then dropped it. Syracuse's Tom Marechek swooped down and hurled it in to tie the game.

The defenses took over in the first overtime and neither team was able to score. At the start of the second sudden death period, Princeton's Andy Moe took charge. Claiming the face-off, he stormed through the Syracuse defense and powered the ball past the lunging Surran for the winning goal.

Happy to have broken the championship monopoly of Syracuse, North Carolina, and Johns Hopkins, Princeton captain Mike Mariano said, "Dynasties are boring." But he did not mind that the Tigers went on to establish their own dynasty, winning the NCAA title in 1994, '96, and '97, when they posted a perfect 15–0 regular season record. Their success helped the ancient game of lacrosse reach new heights of popularity from elementary schools to professional and inter-national levels.

2

LITTLE BROTHER
OF WAR

Ball and stick games go back as far as recorded history. Nobody knows when or where one of these games became lacrosse. "It's closely related to a lot of ball games that we find remnants of in Mexico and South America," explained Syracuse University's lacrosse coach Roy Simmons Jr. "There are ball courts in architectural ruins, but we really don't understand how the game was played."

The earliest accounts of the sport identify it with the Indians of North America. Native American tribes traced the origins of the game to various myths. An Ojibwa tale told of a boy's dream that explained how the game should be played. The Menominee attributed its invention to a story concerning an avenged death.

One of the best known Indian legends, "How the Bat Got Its Wings," tells of a mythical lacrosse game held between a team of animals and a team of birds. The story focuses on how the bat was to be classified; was it a bird or an animal? The birds believed that any creature having teeth should play for the animals, while the animals declared that any flying creature was a bird.

To Native American tribes, lacrosse was a religious ritual, a way to settle disputes, and a training ground for young warriors. The games covered many miles and several days.

When the animals sent the bat to the feathered team, the birds rejected him. They sent the bat to play with the animals, who finally relented, allowing the bat to join their side for the game.

During the contest the birds quickly took the lead because of the crane's ability to slowly move the ball in the air. The crane's advantage gave the animals the idea to use the bat for the same purpose. He quickly proved to be speedier and more agile than the large crane. After the bat led the animals to victory, they agreed that the small creature with teeth should be classified as an animal.

Many important details of lacrosse as played by the North American Indians have been preserved by legends and oral histories. Others came from 18th century French Jesuit priests, who had come as missionaries to the region of Quebec in Canada once known as New France. Jesuits were trained to observe the most minute aspects of a culture; they carefully recorded their observations in diaries.

During the 19th century American artist George Catlin provided the most important visual record of lacrosse before the introduction of photography in the latter part of that century. Catlin's detailed paintings filled in gaps not found in oral histories or the Jesuits' diaries.

A primary function of lacrosse was to train young warriors for battle. Ruth Underlie, a historian of Native Americans, reported that the Cherokee tribe referred to the game as "little brother of war."

Early lacrosse was a lengthy, rough, and occasionally violent sport designed to develop strength and endurance. Players underwent strenuous training in preparation for important games. Fasting was often a part of such training, since combat usually required that warriors go without food for long periods of time. If young men were permitted any food prior to matches, it did not include the meat of any animal considered to be easily injured, weak, or timid.

The game was even used as a war strategy. When Chief Pontiac wanted to capture a French fort in what is now Michigan, his warriors could not get near the walls. The chief and his braves staged a ball game with the French looking on. Soon, the Frenchmen realized that the ball was gradually getting closer to the fort. Suddenly Chief Pontiac gave the signal; the Indians jumped the wall and captured the fort.

Lacrosse games were also used to settle major conflicts between communities or tribes. Historian Frances Wyman wrote, "Sometimes contested land titles or the arbitration of a bitter quarrel depended on the outcome; the winner prevailed. As an alternative to armed

Indian lacrosse games often had hundreds of players on each side. There were few rules and no protective equipment, so injuries were common.

conflict, lacrosse was far better, for at worst it was no more dangerous than football."

According to American Indian lacrosse author Thomas Vennum Jr. "Any number of physical maneuvers that today would draw fouls were permitted: tackling, wrestling, tripping, charging, ramming, slashing, and striking with the stick. Some of the actions were controlled but with only minimal regulations." Indians wore no protective gear such as face masks or helmets, so injuries were common.

Women were not allowed to play lacrosse. Instead they enjoyed other popular games, including shinny, a ball-and-stick game resembling field hockey. But females participated in lacrosse in other ways. If any player became weary and his aggressiveness lessened, women emerged from the sidelines and flogged him with sticks until he resumed spirited play. Women also cheered and offered support to their favorite warriors.

Wagering on games was a common practice, and flogging was used to improve the chances of winning a bet. A George Catlin painting shows a Choctaw woman entering the woods to get materials for the "whip." She hoists her skirts while running onto the field, yelling and screaming, trying to catch her husband to remind him of all the goods they had bet on the game. Catlin wrote, "She lashes him over the naked shoulders, and often to the degree that the blood will be seen trickling down over his back."

Unlike today's teams of seven players, early lacrosse was often a mass game of 100 or more. Sometimes as many as 1,000 players participated. A game might last two or three days, with play halted when it got too dark, then resuming at sunrise. During long games entire teams of replacement players relieved their exhausted teammates every 15 minutes or so.

Indian lacrosse fields were located near streams so players could refresh themselves during games, and close to villages for convenience and safety. If an enemy attacked during a game, the tribe could rush to the safety of palisaded walls that surrounded some villages. Visiting teams often camped on the lacrosse field during the night.

The players first cleared the field of stones and rocks, using deer- or moose-antler hoes. They did a good job, since they often played barefoot. In some parts of the country, spring rains saturated playing surfaces, turning them

Winter didn't stop northern tribes like the Sioux, who played lacrosse on frozen lakes.

into muddy mires. Many Northern tribes played on the frozen surfaces of lakes during the winter, wearing moccasins.

The distance between goals usually varied from 500 yards to half a mile; however, goals could be located several miles apart. There were no sidelines; at times players roamed over the land in all directions.

Goals might have been a single tree, a pole, or a rock. When the ball hit the goal, a score was earned. Some tribes played with two goal posts situated six to nine feet apart with scores made by the ball passing between the posts.

Many tribes painted their bodies red to signify combat. Some placed decorative feathers in their hair from birds of prey, believing the feathers gave them the keen eyesight of a hawk or the skills to attack like an eagle. They also rubbed various forms of grease on their skin so that opposing players had difficulty gripping them.

The Indians used several varieties of lacrosse balls: light balls of stuffed deerskin or similar animal hide, or solid balls, usually made from wood. Wooden balls were rarely found among southeastern tribes, who used

A Passamaquoddy racket and ball. The ball was made of a single piece of hide with a thong drawstring.

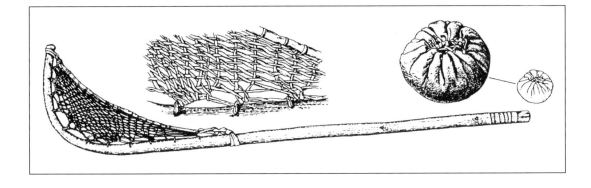

deerskin spheres and fragile sticks. But tribes from other regions often used a knot of wood from a tree. Other tribes used clay balls covered with hides. Hide-covered balls were made in several sizes. In *Travels* (1776–78) Jonathan Carver described the lacrosse balls of the Great Lakes region as slightly bigger than tennis balls.

Balls constructed from hides were bag-shaped and closed with a type of drawstring, then sewn shut with animal sinew. The Mohawk and Choctaw formed balls by tightly interweaving strips of hide over a stuffed center. Biographer William Stone described the Iroquois as using a ball "formed of a network, woven of thongs of untanned deer-skin, strained to the tension of tight elasticity." These balls were moistened so that the outer covering shrank around the ball's stuffing.

Some tribes used a ball about the size of a golf ball, stuffed with moss, bear sinews, tightly woven yarn, punk (which might be decayed wood), roe skins (from a roe deer, similar to an antelope) or woolen rags.

Tribes such as the Ojibwa used hard wooden balls made from a tree's knot. The small fist of wood was charred and the burnt portion scraped away to shape the ball. The Ojibwa also carved perfectly round wooden balls from the wood of willow trees.

Lacrosse sticks also varied from tribe to tribe and region to region. The oldest known stick dates back to the 1820s and is exhibited at the Beltrami Museum in Italy, a museum named for the explorer who traveled to northern Minnesota and observed the game being played.

Some lacrosse sticks had pockets completely enclosed by wood; others had unenclosed pockets. An 18th-century historian compared them to a "racquet or hurl, which is an implement of very curious construction, somewhat resembling a ladle or little hoop net." Some Indians measured the distance from the player's fingertips to the ground when his arms were at his sides to customize the stick's dimensions for an individual.

Lacrosse sticks were adorned with feathers or brightly colored pieces of cloth. Occasionally designs were burned or etched in the sticks' handles, but because the sticks were often broken, many players did not invest their time in etching them. Some designs represented Native American symbols, such as the Ojibwa's serrated grooves that also adorned their drums and war rattles. The Indians adopted symbols introduced by Christian missionaries. According to Victoria Lindsay Levine and James H. Howard's *Choctaw Music and Dance*, the St. Andrew's cross was a commonly used design since it meant, "May our paths cross again and again."

Strands of lacing inserted through holes in the cup formed a pocket. The net was made of twisted bark or leather. The Iroquois used a taut webbing, an important factor in handling the stick. Gradually, the Iroquois style of stick changed to utilize a deeper or "true" pocket to facilitate cradling the ball.

Tribes from the Southeast, Great Lakes, and the St. Lawrence lowlands regions played with enclosed pocket sticks used singly (in one hand) as well as paired sticks (one held in each hand). Tribes using paired sticks included some Iroquois, the Creek, Choctaw, Cherokee, Seminole, and Yuchi. Paired sticks were shorter than single sticks, averaging 2 to 2 $^1/_2$ feet.

In the double-stick game, players carried the ball cupped between the two pockets. The paired sticks were carried close to the body to control and guard the ball. (A warrior might even cup the ball in both sticks and carry them down the field in one hand.) One stick was made slightly shorter than the other, making them easier to manipulate. The shorter stick's net pocket was made slightly smaller than the other, so that they nested while being carried or stored.

The unenclosed single stick was used by Indians in the Northeast in both Canada and the United States. Tribes such as the Algonquian, some Iroquois, and the Passamaquoddy used this style, which was adopted by non-Indian players in Montreal, and evolved into the modern stick used by today's high school and college teams. This style of play required both hands to control a single stick.

The stick's net was bagged to catch and hold the ball. The net's tautness permitted the ball to be thrown, but the web's slack tension made it difficult to quickly throw the small sphere. Therefore, Indians preferred carrying the ball, seldom passing. They observed one strict rule: the ball could not be touched by a player's hands. This was considered a foul. The Cherokee word for such an infraction was uwa'yi—"with the hand."

Even during daylong matches, the ball seldom touched the ground. In 1828, an English traveler noted a Creek game in Alabama where a young warrior took the ball

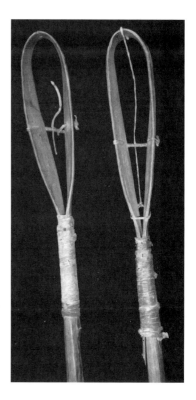

Early sticks had no nets. Some tribes carved ornate designs into the handles and decorated them with feathers or colored cloth.

An illustration in Harper's *magazine may depict an early game between Indians and non-Indians. Players on one team appear to be wearing hats.*

between two sticks, the style of lacrosse played by his tribe: "At length an Indian, more expert than the others, continued to nip the ball between the ends of two sticks, and, having managed to fork it out, ran off with it like a deer, with his arms raised over his head, pursued by the whole party engaged in the first struggle."

At times a game began after the ball was thrown in the air by a chief as the teams assembled in midfield. On other occasions teams stood at opposite ends of the field as a young maiden placed the ball in midfield. At a signal, players rushed to the center where the ball was placed in play.

No one knows how the modern face-off evolved as a means of beginning a game. But in 1797 an eyewitness to a Seneca-Mohawk match reported Native Americans using this practice. Two sides arranged themselves in parallel lines facing one another while a beautiful maiden placed the ball in the center. Two opposing players advanced "and with united bats raised it from the ground to such an elevation as gave a chance for a fair stroke," wrote an observer.

The Native American game remained unchanged until French missionaries became active in the sport. Gradually, as non-Indians picked it up, they changed the rules and style of play, leading to the modern game.

LACROSSE
AND RELIGION

Many sports originated as religious ceremonies. The ancient Greek poet Homer told of the Greek god, Apollo, being directly responsible for success in sporting events.

Lacrosse was an important part of many Native American religious ceremonies. Like other ancient civilizations, the games of the Native Americans were deeply rooted in religious beliefs and legends. The various tribes had no single religion just as they had no single language, but many shared certain beliefs. One was the existence of a magic, mysterious force in nature—spirit power—that was superior to humans and capable of controlling their lives. Members of the Algonquian tribes called the spirit manito, the Iroquois called it orenda, and the Sioux called it wokonda.

Many ceremonies focused on petitioning some god or spirit's help in the production of a bountiful crop or a hunt.

Lacrosse games were organized as part of religious holidays timed to coincide with changes of season or the appearance of heavenly bodies. For instance, the Oklahoma Creek held a special lacrosse match that was part of their Green Corn Ceremony to mark summer's end. The Abenaki claimed that the northern lights (the aurora borealis) signaled a lacrosse game played by their ancestors who lived in the heavens.

The Cayuga Indians believed in the existence of seven thunder gods who played in thunderhead

Indians paid as much attention to their game apparel as to their equipment. This brave is ready for the two-stick version of the game.

clouds where a bolt of lightning represented their ball. They held a one-day ceremony in midwinter between the tribe's young and older men to appeal to their grandfathers (ancestors) for continued service to man. In *Lacrosse and the Cayuga Thunder Rite*, author Frances Eyman wrote, "To honor the seven thunder gods, each team usually had seven players on a side, their goals were laid seven paces wide, and seven points were required to win."

Lacrosse was rooted in such legends. Indians believed that a game's outcome was predestined by spirits who placed more importance on religious leaders than on individual athletes. These tales, explaining events that were believed to be determined by spirits, gods, and ancestors, were handed down from father to son.

Native American ceremonies often focused on hunting and farming, since tribes were totally dependent on these activities for obtaining food. The purpose of such ceremonies was to petition some god or spirit's help in the production of a bountiful crop or a good hunt.

Lacrosse games were a part of funerals or memorial services for famous players. During these sacred ceremonies players held their sticks to represent playing with the honored man for the final time. Gifted lacrosse players were buried with their sticks for play in the afterworld, a practice that endures today, resembling the ancient Egyptians' custom of burying Pharaohs with their scepters.

Matches were also used to settle tribal disputes. According to Alexander M. Weyland and Milton R. Roberts in *The Lacrosse Story*,

"Since lacrosse was a sacred game, played under the watchful eyes of [the] god[s] and chance, it served as a rite to invoke the aid of the gods on the side of the right. Gaming is often a ritual of divination or a trial of justice."

Indians believed that a religious practitioner or a shaman was needed to communicate with the spirit. These shamans were also referred to as medicine men since their powers included abilities to cure the sick. Medicine men could be hired by individuals, family groups, or even lacrosse teams.

The feathers of an eagle were believed to impart the bird's qualities of keen eyesight and swift powerful motion to the player who wore them. This medicine man is preparing to pluck the feathers of a dead eagle.

Lacrosse games were even held as "curing ceremonies." In 1636 a French missionary reported that such games were the most important medicinal rite among the Huron Indians in Canada. The full participation of all tribe members in a pregame dance was believed essential for a successful cure. In addition to shamans, religious priests served to conduct public ceremonies, but they did not perform medical cures.

Although medicine men did not play in lacrosse games, their services were considered necessary. Teams routinely paid priests and medicine men who were believed to possess the powers to control players through the use of magical spells and symbols. These practitioners might be paid with money (many Indians used a form of currency made from colored beads known as wampum), clothing, cloth, or tobacco. The shamans were hired before a game, and such pay was called a "toe hold" since the medicine man was to give the team an advantage.

Magical devices used to weaken the opposition included a doll made from the roots of a plant known as beggar's-lice, whose stems resembled human figures. Many Native Americans believed that these dolls bewitched opponents; they gave the figures the names of rival teams or players.

Shamans and priests conducted elaborate ceremonies prior to lacrosse games. Some tribes, such as the Iroquois, fasted and bathed prior to a game. The Cherokee held a pregame ritual they called "going to water" in which players stood by a river or stream. Each man held his lacrosse stick before him while the priest prayed over red beads for success and black beads to weaken the opposition. The ceremony ended when each player dipped his stick in the water before touching it to his lips to increase the stick's power. According to author Thomas Vennum in *American Indian Lacrosse: Little Brother of War*, as the sticks were immersed, a priest recited a verse: "This is to Doctor the Ball Sticks to be able to Pick up the Ball."

Pregame purification rituals among such tribes as the Yuchi, Ojibwa, and Creek required players to drink potions or emetics which caused vomiting, making them "pure." Vennum reports, "They followed the emetic with a sweat bath to further purify and strengthen them."

The Creek, Menominee, and Choctaw were some of the tribes whose players rubbed ointments on their skin prior to games for strength and skill. Southeastern tribes such as the Yuchi, Creek, and Cherokee used a surgical instrument to scratch a player's skin before play. These tribes believed scratching to bring blood to the skin's surface resulted in cleansing and increased endurance.

Medicine men officiated at games, blessed equipment, directed ceremonies, and prescribed game strategy and dress. They kept score by using tally sticks on which scores were notched with knives.

Tribes who used wooden balls, such as the Ojibwas' willow sphere, often engraved the balls with symbolic carvings: circles, stars, and crosses. Other tribes painted the balls; the Menominee used two colors, red and black. Many tribes elaborately painted a player's body prior to lacrosse matches.

No English, a Peoria shaman in 1830, is shown holding a prayer stick. The shamans played a large role in the rituals surrounding lacrosse.

The shamans "doctored the balls." Some tribes used balls made of the skins of certain animals, which had to be killed in a specified manner. Balls were stuffed with various secret materials thought to hold magical powers, such as animals or birds whose characteristics held special significance. For instance, anthropologist John R. Swanton reported that the Creek Indians used inchworms to stuff a "chief ball." The Creek believed inchworms were invisible to birds, making it difficult for the opponents to see the ball.

Lacrosse sticks were blessed before games with music and dancing in which the women were allowed to participate. Shamans often rubbed the sticks with special ointments, and adorned them with feathers. They decorated sticks with paint, and carved or burned special symbols on them. The Cherokee used diamond markings representing the rattlesnake, since it was believed that the reptile attacked quickly and held the power to charm its prey. A jagged line represented a lightning bolt, empowering the stickman to strike swiftly.

During play, medicine men were believed to possess the ability to control players and equipment through the use of magical spells. A Cherokee shaman placed a bull turtle's hide in a dish behind his team's goal to bring the ball "home." The Cherokee also believed that if a team's shaman stood behind their goal, he held the power to attract a ball stuffed with an inchworm. These shamans waged symbolic battles against the magic of each other's medicine, "fighting" to create a spell more potent than their opponent's.

Playing fields were also oriented in accordance with religious beliefs. Because the Cherokee believed water to be sacred, their fields were located near rivers or streams. The Ojibwa aligned fields east to west, adhering to their beliefs about the sun's path.

The Native American game of lacrosse was and remains an important and fascinating aspect of their rich and ancient culture. Understanding the complex nature of Indian religious beliefs is vital to fully appreciating how the sacred game has been intricately woven into their lives in both the past and present.

THE MODERN GAME

If members of ancient North American Indian tribes returned to earth to witness a modern lacrosse game, they might recognize fundamental parts of the early sport. But the game has changed drastically in many ways.

Canada was the first country to show great interest in lacrosse. When the Dominion of Canada was created on July 1, 1867, lacrosse was declared the country's national sport. Dr. William George Beers, a Montreal-born dentist and a devoted student of the game, formed the Canadian National Lacrosse Association that year. Dr. Beers, who had played lacrosse since age six, was a gifted organizer who vigorously promoted the game.

After careful study and analysis of the ancient sport, Dr. Beers concluded that lacrosse should emphasize team play. He revised the game to reflect that philosophy and drew up the sport's first official set of rules. A summary of the major regulations follows.

Team: A team consisted of 12 men with the following positions: goalkeeper, point, cover point, center, home, and fielders.

No substitutions were allowed after a match began, even if a player was injured.

Match: A match was decided by three goals or "games" out of five unless the captains established other terms. If a team had failed to score three victories by darkness, the match was

(Top) Two players for the 1884 Stevens Institute of Technology team at practice. (Below) These members of the 1944 Stevens team practice on the same field. The rackets and uniforms changed more than the rough-and-tumble game did. Stevens has fielded a lacrosse team for more than 100 years.

called a draw. However, the captains could agree that if one side led 2–0 when darkness fell, they would be the winner.

Goals and length of field: Although Dr. Beers recommended a distance of 200 feet between goals, captains established their own distances. Each post was 6 feet high, crowned by a flag. The posts were situated 6 feet apart.

Goal crease: A line placed 6 feet in front of the goal posts. No opponent was permitted to cross the line until the ball crossed it.

The stick: Any length, with the netting required to lie flat when no ball was in it.

The ball: India rubber sponge not less than 8 inches and not more than 10 inches in circumference.

Coach: Each team had a "field captain" to supervise the play. If not a player, he could not carry a stick.

Officials: Two umpires, one from each side, were stationed at each goal. After an umpire called "Time," the ball could not be touched by either player, nor could players move from the position in which they happened to be at the moment, until the umpire called "Play."

A referee was selected by the umpires. His decision was final, but he was advised to listen to players, umpires, and field captains in the event of a controversial call.

Fouls: Players were not allowed to wear spiked shoes, to hold another player with the stick or hands, to throw a stick at a player or at a ball, or to strike, trip, or threaten. They were not permitted to touch the ball with their hands (except for the goalkeeper, who could block the ball with a hand).

As the American Civil War ended in 1865, soldiers returned to their homes, where they introduced baseball and other sports they had played in military camps. Suddenly, America became a sports-minded country. Exhibition lacrosse games immediately attracted interest.

The sport's popularity spread to Europe. In 1867 an Indian team visited Scotland, Ireland, England, and France. Following their trip, lacrosse clubs formed in England. The English Lacrosse Association adopted a code of laws that differed from the Canadian game in several ways, including establishing the sport's first time limit.

Women began to play as well. However, the first women's lacrosse association, formed in England, was not established until 1912.

Another Indian troupe demonstrated lacrosse at the Saratoga Springs fairgrounds on August 7, 1867, where the sport drew its first mention in an American newspaper. On October 16 of that year, a troupe of Native Americans appeared in an exhibition game held during a baseball tournament in Troy, New York. The next day the Indians played a lacrosse match against a team of baseball players. The *Troy Daily Times* reported, "Thousands gained admission and several hundred saw the game from the hills to the east." The match led to formation of the first American lacrosse club, the Mohawk Club of Troy.

In 1868 a game was played in New York City, where the *New York Tribune* reported, "Lacrosse may be called a madman's game, so wild it is." After these exhibition games, lacrosse clubs sprang up in the North, East,

Dr. William Beers promoted lacrosse in Canada and drew up the sport's first official set of rules.

An Onondaga team c. 1900. Indian teams playing exhibitions of the sport helped to spread its popularity in the Northeast.

and Midwest. An unusual experiment took place in Ottawa on August 18, 1868—"Fire ball" lacrosse. This novel idea was designed to make playing and viewing the game at night possible, but the concept quickly went up in flames. When the ball was saturated with turpentine and ignited, the fastenings burned, causing the ball to fall apart. Not only was the burning ball a problem, the sticks' netting also caught fire.

Exhibition games continued to promote lacrosse around the globe. In 1876 Dr. Beers led an Indian group and a lacrosse club to the British Isles where they played on June 26 before Queen Victoria at Windsor Castle. Following the exhibition, the queen noted the game as "very pretty to watch."

After returning to North America they played before 8,000 spectators at the West-chester Polo Club in Newport, Rhode Island. Said the *New York Herald*: "The immense popular success of the game caused lacrosse to be the talk of Newport. The universal verdict is that lacrosse is the most remarkable, versatile, and exciting of all games of ball."

Intercollegiate lacrosse was born when Manhattan College faced New York University in the fall of 1877. NYU led 2–0 when the game was called because of darkness.

One individual was so influential in promoting lacrosse in the United States that he is called "the father of American lacrosse." John R. Flannery started the movement that led to the formation of the United States National Amateur Lacrosse Association in 1879. As a 16-year-old he represented Montreal's Shamrock Club. Later he resided in Boston, where he helped organize the Union Lacrosse Club. After moving to New York, he joined the Ravenswood Club and enthusiastically promoted the sport until his death in 1919. Flannery's leadership resulted in the creation of nine clubs in New York state.

Eventually, lacrosse spread south of New York to include teams from Baltimore and Princeton. In 1882 the Intercollegiate Lacrosse Association was formed. Yale and Johns Hopkins fielded teams amid the Association's swelling ranks. Across the border, amateur lacrosse flourished in Canada, but the nation's colleges failed to embrace the sport.

In 1889, one former player wrote, "The one objection to lacrosse which has no doubt kept it from becoming a popular game hitherto is

John R. Flannery actively promoted lacrosse, forming clubs in Boston and New York in the 1870s.

the long time it takes to learn to play it well." The Native American game had been designed to train warriors. The development, skill, and endurance lacrosse required resulted from practice over many years.

After dominating the early college game, Yale, Harvard, and Princeton became reluctant to take lacrosse players from their major sports such as football, baseball, rowing, and track. As smaller schools produced quality teams, the Big Three abandoned lacrosse. During the 1890s the sport declined, but as more smaller colleges took up the game, its growth continued throughout the South and Midwest. By the turn of the century, lacrosse rebounded; in 1906 John Flannery called it, "The King of the Field Games."

College players transformed the game. Johns Hopkins center Ronald Abercrombie introduced the use of a tennis net stretched between the goal posts. Later, Abercrombie initiated the use of a shorter stick. The practice caught on among his Hopkins teammates, resulting in the rise of the sport's short passing game.

During the 1904 Olympic Games in St. Louis, Missouri, an exhibition lacrosse championship took place. None of the famous eastern teams from America or Canada participated, however. In the final game on July 7, Winnipeg, Manitoba's Shamrock Club, the Western Canadian champions, defeated the St. Louis Amateur Athletic Association 8–2. No American team represented the United States in the 1908 Olympic Games held in London.

During World War I, military training consumed much of the students' leisure time. Some American colleges were unable to field lacrosse teams, but when the war ended in 1918, the sport slowly regained its prewar momentum.

At the turn of the century, British women who taught in the United States introduced lacrosse to their students. Miss Rosabelle Sinclair of England began to organize women's clubs near Baltimore in 1926, and women's clubs sprouted in Philadelphia and New York. In 1931 the United States Women's Lacrosse Association was formed. The country's first women's lacrosse championship was played in Greenwich, Connecticut, in 1933.

The Canadian team practices in the Los Angeles Coliseum for a series of games against Johns Hopkins University, representing the U.S. at the 1932 Olympics. Hopkins won two of the three games before the largest crowds ever to watch lacrosse.

Despite its being called "the fastest game on two feet" by Baltimore sportswriter W. Wilson Wingate, the way the game was played and the equipment used remained a mystery to most American sports fans. However, the sport received worldwide publicity when exhibition lacrosse returned to the Olympics in 1928 and 1932. During the 1928 games in Amsterdam the United States was represented by Johns Hopkins, who had defeated the best teams of the U.S. for the honor.

When the 1932 Olympic games were held in Los Angeles, the United States and Canada were the only two countries represented in exhibition lacrosse. Once again the Johns Hopkins stickmen, coached by Dr. Ray Van Orman, earned the right to represent the United States. On August 7, 1932, the first of three scheduled lacrosse games was played. Earlier that day, the 26-mile marathon had begun and many of the 100,000 spectators had gathered to await the finish of that ancient Olympic event. The crowd witnessed an exciting lacrosse game matching Canada against the U.S. squad, who won 5–3.

A three-day total of 145,000 spectators saw the Americans win two of three games behind the outstanding play of Johns Hopkins attackman Jack Turnbull and goalie Fritz Stude. Wingate, editor of the *Lacrosse Guide*, wrote, "The Johns Hopkins twelve of 1932, the American Olympic representative, stands all alone at the top of the list of great lacrosse teams of all time. Never before in the history of lacrosse in the United States has any other stick machine ever gone undefeated and untied through three months of weekly competition against the nation's strongest opponents."

The 1932 Johns Hopkins team had brought the game of lacrosse to the nation's attention in dazzling fashion. It was the beginning of a new and exciting era for the sport.

The most drastic rule changes in the history of modern lacrosse were enacted in 1933. Designed to speed up the game by providing more wide-open play, the rules reduced the number of players from 12 to 10, the distance between goals was reduced from 110 yards to 80 yards, and the playing area in the rear of each goal was fixed at 20 yards.

Modern field lacrosse combines aspects of basketball, soccer, ice hockey, and football. A fast-paced game, it requires cooperation and team play. It is played by boys and girls as well as adults, with variations between men's and women's rules.

Men's lacrosse teams are composed of 10 players: three attackmen, three midfielders, three defensemen, and a goalie. To begin the game, the referee places the ball between the sticks of the two center players, who try to gain possession at the official's signal. The ball is carried in the stick and passed or kicked to get it into the opponent's goal. Opposing players may block one another. After each goal the team scored upon gets possession of the ball at midfield.

Players move the ball by carrying it with the stick, passing it with a wrist-flipping motion, or kicking it. The goalie is the only player allowed to use his hands to stop shots at the goal.

Fouls are classified as technical or personal. Technicals are less serious than personals, with

The ball is moved by carrying it with the stick, passing it, or kicking it, without using the hands. Here a Navy attackman prepares to flip the ball to a teammate while two Rutgers defenders close in on him.

penalties ranging from a 30-second suspension to the loss of possession to the other team.

Referees decide the severity of a personal foul, which could result in a one-minute or longer suspension up to expulsion from the game. Personal fouls involve unsportsmanlike conduct, checking an opponent with the portion of the stick held between the hands, illegal body checking (hitting an opponent from the rear, below the knees, or above the shoulders when he or she is not in possession of the ball), slashing (striking a player on any part of the body other than the gloved hand or stick), or tripping.

Box lacrosse is played in hockey arenas with six players on each side. In 1975 National Lacrosse League box lacrosse was introduced in New England in this game between the Boston Bolts and the New York Tomahawks.

Men's lacrosse games are 60 minutes long, divided into four 15-minute periods. Tie games are decided by sudden death overtime play. The field is 110 yards long and 60 to 70 yards wide. Each goal is centered in an 18-foot circle called the goal crease. The goals have 6-foot-square openings with net backings and are 80 yards apart.

Women's teams have 12 players. Their playing fields have no sideline limits, but are usually bounded by the topography surrounding the field. Games are 50 minutes long, divided into halves with a 10-minute intermission.

Box lacrosse is popular in some regions, especially Canada. It is played in hockey arenas with six players on a side. Its continuous action and physical contact make it similar to ice hockey. American professional lacrosse is played indoors.

Modern lacrosse balls are made from India rubber. They are slightly smaller than baseballs and may be white or orange. Until the 1960s the sticks were made of wood, in two parts— the handle and the head. Today more sticks are plastic, with lightweight molded plastic heads on shafts of aluminum or wood. The net in the stick head is made of nylon and serves the same purpose as the pocket in a baseball glove. The rules require that the depth of the pocket or net shall not exceed the width of the ball. At eye level, the entire ball must be seen below the bottom of the stick's sidewall.

Sticks range from 40 to 72 inches long and $6^{1}/_{2}$ to 10 inches wide; attackers usually use shorter sticks than defensemen.

Most players wear uniforms consisting of a shirt and shorts; many players wear protective

Two women battle for the ball in an Australian tournament. Women's teams have 12 players; their fields have no marked sidelines.

padding as well. Shoes are cleated for play on grass fields; sneakers are usually worn on artificial surfaces. Each player is required to wear a mouthpiece, face mask, protective helmet, and padded gloves that cover every finger.

Changes in the rules and the use of lighter equipment resulted in new styles of play. Improved stick heads simplified ball handling, making scoring easier. The sticks' lighter shafts increased defenders' ability to check an opponent by attempting to dislodge the ball from the stick head. The faster action and higher scoring inspired veteran sportswriter

Grantland Rice to observe, "Once in a while they argue about the fastest game—hockey or basketball, then about the roughest game—boxing, football, the all-star combination of speed and body contact. [Lacrosse] requires more elements of skill than any game I know."

The modern game also fostered the emergence of a galaxy of legendary superstars.

6

THE GAME'S GREATEST PLAYERS

The stories of lacrosse's greatest players are often family stories. At the top of the roll are the Turnbull brothers and the Gait twins.

Doug and Jack Turnbull and their two sisters inherited their athletic skills from their father, Doug Sr. One of the finest all-around amateur athletes in Maryland history, Doug Sr. played football, baseball, cricket, tennis, and golf, and was a boxer, wrestler, swimmer, hunter, and fisherman.

Born in Baltimore, Doug Jr. began playing lacrosse at the age of 10, when there were 12 players on a side. In 1922 he launched a four-year career at Johns Hopkins, in which he played every position except goalie and made the All-American team four times. He also played football, leading the nation in place-kicking in 1923.

After graduating, Doug played 13 years for the Mt. Washington Club of Baltimore, one of the top club teams in the country. He was named to the Hall of Fame in 1963.

At a dinner honoring past Hopkins lacrosse captains, he heard a poem that summarized his life in the game:

> Give a boy a stick he can hold
> Give a boy a ball he can toss
> And you've given him something
>   that's better than gold—
> The pleasure of playing lacrosse.

Gary Gait, a four-time All-American at Syracuse, went on to star in the Major Indoor Lacrosse League, where he made all-pro seven times and was the league MVP three times. Here he carries the ball for the Baltimore Thunder of the National Lacrosse League in 1998.

Doug Turnbull Jr. may be the greatest lacrosse player ever, but he would give his vote to his younger brother Jack. "It didn't take me very long to teach him all that I knew," Doug said.

Born John Inglehardt Turnbull in 1910, Jack became known as "the Babe Ruth of lacrosse." As a schoolboy he competed in swimming and track meets; in high school he played football, basketball, lacrosse, and ice hockey. He played midfield and attack

Jack Turnbull is called "the Babe Ruth of lacrosse." He and his brother Doug starred in high school, at Johns Hopkins, and on the national champion Mt. Washington Club team of Baltimore.

for the Mt. Washington Club before enrolling at Hopkins in 1929. Although he stood under 5' 8", for the next three years he starred as a tailback for the football team and attackman on the lacrosse team, which he captained in 1932, their second consecutive undefeated season.

In a tournament held to decide the United States team for the 1932 Olympics, Turnbull scored three goals on six shots in Hopkins' 7–5 win for the trip to Los Angeles. In 1936 he was a member of the American field hockey team at the Olympic Games in Berlin.

From 1933 to 1942 Jack and Doug played for the Mt. Washington Wolfpack.

While still a student, Jack had learned to fly. When World War II began, he enlisted in the Army Air Corps and became a bomber pilot flying missions over Germany. On October 18, 1944, his plane was returning from a mission when it ran into a storm and collided with another bomber. Turnbull was killed in the crash.

To honor Jack Turnbull, the Attackman of the Year award in each division is named for him.

In 1987 the Gait twins came out of the Canadian Northwest and revolutionized the game of lacrosse. Drawn by the chance to play in the Carrier Dome and for coach Roy Simmons Jr., Paul and Gary Gait came to Syracuse from British Columbia and brought a wide-open run-and-gun style to the game. After losing in the semifinals of the NCAA tournament their first year, they began a three-year domination of the field that culminated in a 1990 team called the best ever.

Gary Gait (left) and his twin brother Paul led Syracuse to three straight national championships, 1988–90. Their wide-open, acrobatic style revolution- ized the game.

After an undefeated 1988 season, they faced an underdog University of Pennsylvania team in the NCAA semifinals. People who saw that game still shake their heads in awe. They talk of it as not only the greatest lacrosse game they ever saw, but the most spectacular one-man performance in history.

Early in the game Gary Gait made a play nobody had ever seen. Coming up behind the net, he soared through the air and dunked the ball over the top of the goal. The shot that became known as "Air Gait" stunned the crowd of 11,827. But he didn't stop there. As if to prove that the crowd could believe what it had seen, he repeated the feat.

In all, Gary Gait scored a postseason record nine goals that day. But it almost wasn't enough. Penn led the heavily favored Orangemen 10–9 with a minute to play. Their backs to the wall, Syracuse scrambled to score the tying goal. Then it was Paul Gait's turn.

The Penn coach later described the last seconds of the game. "It was as though Paul looked at the scoreboard clock, saw that there were five seconds left in the game, and said, 'Oh, yeah, the game's tied. I'd better score a goal.' He did just that with three seconds left and Syracuse won, 11–10."

They went on to beat Cornell, 13–8, for the first of three straight national championships. (The 1990 title was later nullified because the coach's wife had co-signed a car loan for Paul Gait that made him an ineligible player.)

Gary Gait was a four-time All-American; Paul was named three times. Between them they set scoring records and turned more new fans on to lacrosse than anyone of their time. During the 1980s, national lacrosse participation doubled.

Coaches have left indelible marks on the game as well. Through 1997 the name Simmons had been associated with lacrosse at Syracuse University for 75 years.

In 1922 Roy Simmons came out of Chicago to play football at Syracuse. He knew nothing about lacrosse when he arrived; the first time he saw a stick he thought it was a crabbing net. Lacrosse was not a major sport. Players

Roy Simmons Sr. (right) and Roy Jr. have been associated with lacrosse at Syracuse for more than 75 years. Roy Jr. succeeded his father as head coach.

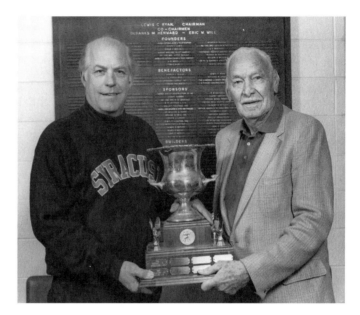

wore the football team's throwaway jerseys. Even 40 years later only one athletic scholarship was allotted to the lacrosse team.

As a quarterback, Simmons led the football team to an 8–1–1 record and its first national championship. He became interested in lacrosse when that team compiled a 17–0 record. He signed up and became a two-time All-American defenseman on two national championship teams.

Simmie, as he was best known, stayed on at the upstate New York campus as a boxing coach, assistant football coach, and head lacrosse coach, retiring in 1970 with a 251–130–1 lacrosse record.

But Simmie's influence was measured by something more than the record book. His players respected and admired him; he was straightforward, sincere, and a stickler for fundamentals. At a time when Native Americans and black athletes were rarities on college teams, Simmons treated all races equally and played the best athletes who tried out. One of those was Jim Brown, the Hall of Fame football player who starred at lacrosse in high school and college.

"I played for Roy Simmons, the only coach at Syracuse who was good to me from the day I arrived," Brown said. "My size in lacrosse was uncommon, gave me a huge advantage.

Pro football Hall of Famer Jim Brown's size and speed made him a devastating midfielder on the lacrosse field for Syracuse.

I [weighed] 225 my senior year [1957], playing midfield, where most guys were small. With my bulk, and ability to match their speed, I could pretty much do what I wanted. We didn't lose a game my senior year. The starters would play a quarter, beat a team to death, Simmons would pull us, let the subs play."

An Onondaga chief, Oren Leons, was an All-American goalie and a boxer under Simmons. "If there was a legend," Leons said, "he was it."

Johns Hopkins' Bob Scott was just 24 when he took the helm of the Blue Jays' lacrosse team in 1953, after starring as a midfielder at the University of Virginia. Scott led Hopkins to six USILA titles—including four in a row 1967–70—and the NCAA Championship in 1974, during his 20-year tenure at Hopkins.

The procedure for selecting national championship tournament participants changed in 1971, but not before Cornell coach Richie Moran and the Big Red stickmen endured a humiliating tournament snub the year before. The feisty lacrosse coach had led his Cornell team to an undefeated season in 1970. But the U.S. Intercollegiate Lacrosse Association—the governing body of the sport—named three other teams as co-national champions, despite each of them having lost one game.

So nobody was happier than Moran to see the NCAA take over the sport in 1971, launching an annual tournament to decide the national title on the field. The Cornell Big Red responded by winning that first play-off. Led by Al Rimmer, a Toronto native playing in borrowed sneakers because his shoes had been stolen, the Big Red left no doubt they deserved the number one spot by routing Maryland, 12–6, in the finals.

Moran's teams won national titles in 1976 and '77, winning an NCAA Division 1 record 42 consecutive games during a three-year span. Moran retired in 1997 after 29 years and a 257–121 record.

Collegiate lacrosse is divided into three divisions. Overshadowed by the bigger schools, some Division II and III teams have created enviable though little-publicized dynasties of their own.

Beginning in 1974, Hobart College in Geneva, New York, went to six consecutive NCAA Division II tournaments, then switched to Division III and went to 15 more in a row, winning 15 of the 21. Coach David Urick led them to 10 of their 12 consecutive titles 1980–91, playing before crowds that rarely topped 4,000. In a 37–1 win over MIT, the 1980 team set Division III records for most goals in a game; fewest goals allowed; assists (24); and shots on goal (106). They set tournament records that year with 223 shots on goal and 69 scores in three games.

Urick also coached the U.S. team to the World Games Championship in 1986.

Other schools with long histories of winning teams include Adelphi of Long Island in Division II, and Division III powerhouses Washington College (Maryland), Salisbury State University (Maryland), Ohio Wesleyan, and Nazareth College of Rochester, New York, winners of the 1996–97 championships.

Nazareth's Terry Goetz reacts after scoring the game-winning goal in sudden death overtime as the Golden Flyers defeated Washington College, 11–10, in the 1996 Division III title game. Nazareth repeated with another overtime win over Washington College in 1997. Many small schools have carved out impressive records in lacrosse competition.

7 A FAST-GROWING SPORT

As the 20th century ended, lacrosse showed signs of increasing worldwide interest. Outside of the United States, the game was played in Australia, New Zealand, Canada, England, Wales, Scotland, France, Japan, Hong Kong, Singapore, Germany, Sweden, and the Czech Republic. International tournaments for men's and women's teams became annual events.

But despite its fast pace and spectacular plays, lacrosse continued to lag far behind other major professional sports in television exposure, publicity, and attendance. Salaries remained minuscule compared to the multimillion dollar payrolls of baseball, football, basketball, and hockey.

After 11 years of professional box lacrosse, the Major Indoor Lacrosse League faced a competitor in 1997—the National Lacrosse League. Rather than engage in a costly fight for markets and players, the two leagues merged, starting the 1998 season under the National name. Initial plans put teams in eight northeastern markets.

Club lacrosse, the only way for most college players to remain active in the sport, was played only for the love of the action. The 1997 championship, played on June 14 in Syracuse between Long Island Hofstra and Baltimore-based Chesapeake Toyota, drew 150 spectators despite the presence of former Syracuse stars Paul and Gary Gait and Tom Marechek.

Despite its fast pace and spectacular action, professional lacrosse has struggled to draw the publicity and attendance needed to prosper and grow. Here two teams go up for the ball in a game in a short-lived pro league in the 1970s.

Brigham Young University won the first Collegiate Club championship in 1997, defeating UC Santa Barbara. Club lacrosse is growing on and off college campuses. Here BYU's Rex Hardy launches into the crease to score against UCSB goalie Colby Boysen.

But all that could change as the game's popularity exploded from the college level down to elementary schools.

More than 73,000 fans attended the weekend of NCAA men's championship play in 1997 at the University of Maryland. New college leagues and divisions sprang up. The University of Maryland women's team won their third consecutive championship, although their 50-game winning streak ended in 1997.

In addition to varsity teams, club teams were formed on campuses across the country. Leagues formed, leading to the first collegiate national championship, which was won by Brigham Young University of Utah.

At the high school and elementary school levels, thousands of youngsters added lacrosse sticks to their stash of soccer balls and baseball gloves. They promised a steady flow of talent for future men's and women's teams, and a base of knowledgeable fans for the club and professional leagues.

The opening of the Lacrosse Foundation and Hall of Fame Museum on the Baltimore campus of Johns Hopkins University in 1991 gave the sport a new platform from which to educate the public and promote itself.

Lacrosse has come a long way from the 1930s, when there were only 43 colleges, 24 clubs, and 31 secondary schools playing the sport. But it has not left its Indian roots behind: the six-nation Iroquois Confederacy team is a member of today's International Lacrosse Federation.

CHRONOLOGY

1636   A French missionary sees the Huron Indians playing lacrosse near Thunder Bay, Ontario, and becomes the first to document the game.

1834   Reports of a group of Indians demonstrating lacrosse for men from Montreal appear in the newspaper.

1844   The first documented game between whites and Indians takes place.

1856   The Montreal Lacrosse Club is formed.

1860   Canadian dentist Dr. William Beers begins codifying rules for lacrosse.

1877   New York University fields the nation's first college lacrosse team.

1879   John R. Flannery earns the title "father of American lacrosse" by initiating the National Lacrosse Association.

1881   Harvard defeats Princeton, 3–0, in the first collegiate tournament.

1884   Stevens Tech (New Jersey) begins the longest continuous fielding of a team in the U.S.

1890   The first women's lacrosse game is played by students at St. Leonard's School in Scotland.

1898   William H. Maddren and Ronald T. Abercromie of Johns Hopkins originate shorter sticks, which gives rise to the short passing game.

1904   Lacrosse is first played as an Olympic exhibition sport.

1917   The U.S. Naval Academy begins a seven-year undefeated streak. In 1920 they allow only six goals in nine games, still a record.

1921   The offside rule is instituted.

1931   Canadian box lacrosse is created to fill empty ice hockey arenas during the summer.

1933   The number of players on a side is reduced from 12 to 10.

1947   Position names in men's lacrosse are changed to goalkeeper, midfield, attack, and defense.

1967   The United States, represented by the Mt. Washington Lacrosse Club, wins the first world championship.

1971   The NCAA holds its first collegiate championship, with Cornell defeating the University of Maryland, 12–6.

1987   The Major Indoor Lacrosse League begins professional box lacrosse with teams in Baltimore, New York, Philadelphia, and Washington.

1991   The Lacrosse Foundation and Hall of Fame Museum opens at Johns Hopkins University in Baltimore.

1998   The National Lacrosse League merges with the MILL and begins play with eight teams.

2001   Major League Lacrosse holds its first-ever professional player draft for the league's six initial teams.

FAMOUS PLAYERS

The NCAA Men's Lacrosse Committee selected the Top 25 lacrosse players in Division I between 1970 and 1995. Sixty-nine players were nominated by coaches and former coaches.

Midfielders

Gary Gait, Syracuse

Paul Gait, Syracuse

Brad Kotz, Syracuse

Del Dressel, Johns Hopkins

Brendan Schneck, Johns Hopkins

Rick Kowalchuck, Johns Hopkins

Jonathan Reese, Yale

Frank Urso, Maryland

Attackmen

Tim Nelson, Syracuse

Mike O'Neill, Johns Hopkins

Jack Thomas, Johns Hopkins

Mike French, Cornell

Eamon McEneaney, Cornell

Tim Cafaro, Army

Goalies

Mike Federcio, Johns Hopkins

Larry Quinn, Johns Hopkins

Dan MacKesey, Cornell

Scott Bacigalupo, Princeton

Tom Sears, North Carolina

Defensemen

John DeTomasso, Johns Hopkins

Mark Greenberg, Johns Hopkins

Dave Pietramala, Johns Hopkins

Chris Kane, Cornell

Tom Haus, North Carolina

David Morrow, Princeton

FURTHER READING

Green, Tina Sloan and Agnes Bixler Kurtz. *Modern Women's Lacrosse*. Hanover, New Hampshire: ABK Publications, 1989.

Hinkson, Jim. *Lacrosse: Team Strategies*. Los Angeles: Warwick Publishing, 1996.

Scott, Bob. *Lacrosse: Technique and Tradition*. Baltimore: The Johns Hopkins University Press, 1976.

Trafford, Bobbie and Kath Howarth. *Women's Lacrosse: The Skills of the Game*. Wiltshire, England: The Crowood Press, 1989.

Urick, David. *Sports Illustrated Lacrosse: Fundamentals for Winning*. New York: *Sports Illustrated* (Time, Inc.), 1988.

Vennum, Thomas, Jr. *American Indian Lacrosse: Little Brother of War*. Washington: Smithsonian Institution Press, 1994.

Weyland, Alexander M. and Milton R. Roberts. *The Lacrosse Story*. Baltimore: H. & A. Herman, 1965.

LOIS P. NICHOLSON is a native of Sudlersville, Maryland. She holds B.S. and Master of Education degrees from Salisbury State University. She is a school library media specialist at Easton Elementary in Easton, Maryland, where she lives. In addition to *The Composite Guide to Lacrosse*, she has written the following biographies for young readers: *George Washington Carver: Botanist and Ecologist*; *Oprah Winfrey: Entertainer*; *Helen Keller*; *Michael Jackson*; *Ken Griffey, Jr.*; *Casey Stengel*; *Nolan Ryan*; *Booker T. Washington*; *Oprah Winfrey: Talking With America* (Chelsea House); *Cal Ripken, Jr.: Quiet Hero* (Tidewater); *Georgia O'Keeffe* (Lucent); and *Babe Ruth: Sultan of Swat* (Goodwood Press). In addition to writing, Nicholson visits schools and speaks to students and faculties about writing nonfiction.

INDEX